OVERLAP

Originally about [...] to grandmother [...] the pandemic l[...] [...]e complex and somet[...] explores the strange circularity in what feels like a blink in time from being a granddaughter, daughter and mother to becoming a grandmother and to whatever now lies ahead.

The poems are for my grandmothers Harriet and Winifred, who I see as part of an unsung generation. They would perhaps struggle to understand where we are now – but of course would have coped anyway. Just as we all have to.

VB, 11.1.2022

OTHER TITLES FROM THE EMMA PRESS

POETRY PAMPHLETS

how the first sparks became visible, by Simone Atangana Bekono, tr. from Dutch by David Colmer
do not be lulled by the dainty starlike blossom, by Rachael Matthews
With others in your absence, by Zosia Kuczyńska
Sandsnarl, by Jon Stone
This House, by Rehema Njambi
is, thinks Pearl, by Julia Bird
What the House Taught Us, by Anne Bailey

SHORT STORIES

The Secret Box, by Daina Tabūna, tr. from Latvian by Jayde Will
Tiny Moons: A year of eating in Shanghai, by Nina Mingya Powles
Postcard Stories 2, by Jan Carson
Hailman, by Leanne Radojkovich

POETRY ANTHOLOGIES

Second Place Rosette: Poems about Britain
Everything That Can Happen: Poems about the Future
The Emma Press Anthology of Contemporary Gothic Verse
The Emma Press Anthology of Illness

BOOKS FOR CHILDREN

My Sneezes Are Perfect, by Rakhshan Rizwan
The Bee Is Not Afraid of Me: A Book of Insect Poems
Cloud Soup, by Kate Wakeling

ART SQUARES

Menagerie, by Cheryl Pearson, illustrated by Amy Louise Evans
One day at the Taiwan Land Bank
Dinosaur Museum, by Elīna Eihmane
Pilgrim, by Lisabelle Tay, illustrated by Reena Makwana

OVERLAP

POEMS BY VALERIE BENCE

THE EMMA PRESS

*For Ava and Toby and our 'surprise'
due next week.*

☙

THE EMMA PRESS

First published in the UK in 2022 by The Emma Press Ltd.
Poems © Valerie Bence 2022.

All rights reserved.

The right of Valerie Bence to be identified as the author of this work has been asserted in accordance with the Copyright, Designs and Patents Act 1988.

ISBN 978-1-912915-94-1

A CIP catalogue record of this book
is available from the British Library.

Cover design by Amy Louise Evans.

Printed and bound in the UK
by the Holodeck, Birmingham.

The Emma Press
theemmapress.com
hello@theemmapress.com
Birmingham, UK

CONTENTS

French cricket at Grandma's, circa 1960 1
Collusion 2
The man with a hook for a hand 3
Witch 4
The changing nature of friendship 5
Not as posh as I thought we were 6
Unease 7
Choosing a pen 8
Observation 9
The summer of '72 10
Default 12
Piano 13
Overlap 14
Eggs 15
Before the fall 16
On not being a twin 17
Cocktails 18
I must remind myself that this is a good thing ... 19
A grandmother in isolation 20
Red 22
Press me in peat 24

Acknowledgements 26
About the poet 26
About The Emma Press 26

*'Life can only be understood backwards;
but it must be lived forwards'*
Søren Kierkegaard

French cricket at Grandma's, circa 1960

Behind her house at the end of a not-too-salubrious yard,
when the offices in the Nissen huts had closed,
between overgrown allotments and shattered glasshouses
not repaired since the war, we played French cricket.

Our aim: to tire out the twins who made the runs.
I threw a soft ball to her in her floral overall
with stockings rolled down to her ankles,
her one concession to high summer.
She batted each throw effortlessly away
from her unathletic but brave pale legs.

After, when the twins were taken inside,
I would rummage for treasure in the office bins,
find strips of coloured paper, a pink box of index cards,
plastic bindings coiled and sprung, piles of chad
from industrial hole punchers – white and rainbow colours
for confetti in the serious business of doll weddings.

Winifred. She was the age I am now.
She laughed at anything, taught me to wink,
drank tea from a saucer, gave me a whole half-a-crown
if she had a bingo win, let me walk on the too-small-wall
along the canal without holding her hand.

Only now I think of her clearing up after we'd gone,
as I stand at the window, waving them off.

Collusion

From my vantage point under the kitchen table
I watch her knees as she walks by – dimpled,
thick stocking'd in summer and winter,
slippers with holes at the toes,
crossover pinny pockets full of scraps
and peelings for chickens. Grandma Harriet.

We mash tealeaves and bran for the rabbit,
the sweet aroma fogging her glasses, and every day
she scrubs bloody butcher's aprons
for five shillings a week.
We take the clean ones back on the bus,
until the day she faints outside Boots in the rain,
sliding down the wall like in a cartoon,
her wartime hat slipping over her eyes.

Thinking she is dead I run into the chemist's;
a man brings her a glass of water.
Sipping it she squeezes my arm –
Don't tell him   she says, pulling me close.

This will not be difficult, as in all my seven years
he has never spoken to me.

The man with a hook for a hand

At first sign of an approaching storm
Harriet would open the doors – front and back –
so ball lightning could come in and go out unimpeded:
a moving globe of fire she swore she had seen before;
no fulminologist she, but as an old wife
there was little she didn't know.

At thunder's first distant call all mirrors
were turned to face the wall, a habit learned
when a jagged tip of fork lightning earthed itself
through her father's iron hook for a hand
and killed him. My son has his name,
yet no living person knows how or when
the hand which proved his end was lost.

Was it cut or crushed, sliced from his arm
in medical precision, or an agricultural mishap,
plough-scythed or wrenched from his wrist,
or trench-torn in battle as an army lad?
In an old tool box, I find a fork with rusted thread:
one of the attachments he made. I hold it in my hand,
keep it in full view of a window, just in case of a storm.

Witch

The bad winter of '63 brought freezing fog, wind sharp enough
to geld a ram, blizzards that obliterated landmarks
so we couldn't tell where we were on our own road.
Winifred tied a washing line from front door to gatepost.

Hoarfrost sparkled on the inside of windows,
blanked the view, gave rooms an unearthly pallor.
As soon as we went outside ice formed on our eyelashes,
making blinking sharp and interesting.

In those days everyone cleared their doorstep, path
or patch of pavement, no matter how small or expansive.
So children were sent out with broom or shovel to earn
pocket money, and young fathers put their back into it,

and the old woman we thought was a witch in her shawl,
crunching through a week's compacted snow,
struggling with a string bag of provisions,
fell on her untouched icy path. And we laughed.

They say that in the Arctic breath freezes,
crackles   hangs in the air before falling to the ground.
I pull my shawl around my shoulders   pick up my broom.

The changing nature of friendship

Harriet had a best friend for more than thirty years:
all through the war, swapping coupons and borrowing
matches, newspapers, cups of sugar, saving places in queues
even when they didn't know what it was for.
They were always Mrs Taylor and Mrs Clarke.
After her friend's funeral she said
Lovely woman. I wish I'd known her first name.

Not as posh as I thought we were

In the Victorian green-and-white tiled public lavatory
    after we had put our penny in the slot
Mum would hold me, hovering over the seat
    so as not to catch anything   she said –
then she would effect repairs. Keeping stockings in place
    without suspenders was an act of will:
the deft turning of the tops, making a knot then
    tucking it under, into itself.
There   she would say, and delve into her handbag for scent:
    Yardley, Coty L'Aimant, lily-of-the-valley.
A tiny lace-edged handkerchief smelled of lavender
    as she licked a corner, rubbed smudges from my face
then back out we would go into a summer afternoon,
    to run for the bus.

When she was small, my eldest daughter thought
    my mum and the Queen were the same person.
This was disproved when we stood for hours at the OU
    to see the Queen in some sort of ceremony:
a grainy photo captures her bewildered little face,
    seeing her gran and the Queen at the same time
    in the same place.

Unease

I remember the first time worry　　　　　rocked my little world
Thinking about it now　　there had been an almost palpable sense
of unease for days　　　　I felt something in the air
something unspoken between adults　　　　a feeling recognised
a few times since　　now almost permanently in the pit of the stomach
I caught words as they flew by　　　from the Six O'Clock News
in the unusually silent living room　　　where no one thought
to lay a fire and routine　　seemed to have gone out the window

Bay of Pigs and *Cuba* and *Russia*　　made me think of pink pig's snouts
sticking out of the water as they　　swam and played in the sun
and of countries whose stamps were　　as yet　　　uncollected

7

Choosing a pen

It was a big day
when we chose our Osmiroid pens
which we would write with at big school.

Forms were taken home to be signed,
then the dither of choices: one colour
from more than twenty,

plain or marbled, gold or silver clip,
which script for my old name on the barrel –
the first time I would see it written on anything.

My pen was maroon, plain,
my name printed in white. It cost 17/6d,
the extra threepence for marbling a step too far.

It came with its own vocabulary – suction, italic,
nib, blot, quink – and filling without spilling
was a skill retained even now.

It lived in my new pencil case, embroidered
by Winifred, ready for unknown subjects:
Handwriting, Geometry, Latin, Algebra

in an unknown world
where I would learn other words –
like fuck and bugger and bitch.

Observation

When we were young and in impatient love
we would meet at the edge of the old station.
I would arrive first and stand there excited, self-conscious,
back against adverts for Bird's Custard and Babycham,
looking to where you should come running from the bus.

I thought you were late for our every meeting but in fact
you were always early: you would settle yourself behind pillar
or news stand and, concealed by the metal gate,
watch me come running down the stairs,
all short-pleated-skirt, black-eyeliner and bag-of-books.

I would wait and you would watch, and just as I started to move
you would appear, breathless. *Sorry I'm late* you'd say,
beaming as if you knew I would be the mother of your children.
We would kiss, hold hands; you would fold your coat
around my shoulders, as we walked out into the rain.

I was so happy to see you I never realised
you were always coming from the wrong direction.

The summer of '72

Newly married, we lived in Harriet's house
in the same two rooms as my parents had,
where I was born. That summer of *Harvest* and Led Zep,
the French windows – hardly opened since the war –
let overgrown honeysuckle pour into our rooms that smelt
of nothing but sex – when love was feast not famine.

But outside our enclave, Harriet lived like prey;
that atavistic instinct to keep very still. She lived as the servant
she had been at thirteen, ate alone in the cold kitchen;
he in front of the roaring fire she had laid hours before.
I don't know how she stayed upright, breathing every day.
No-one can say I didn't do my duty   she said to me once.

Her strength evaporated in thunderstorms. She would sit
trembling, curtains drawn, mirrors turned to the wall,
Micky's grey muzzle in her lap, and we would hold hands,
waiting for it to be over. Her money had bought the house,
a few hundred pounds left by a Victorian aunt.
I don't think he ever forgave her for that.

He always looked dapper; she never had anything new.
Her one smart frock was from the WRVS the year the buzz
  bomb hit;
there are small blocks of it on my patchwork bedcover.
In that house of silence, the only sound: a crashing plate
as food she'd spent all afternoon cooking flew through the air
when he came home hours late and found an 'error'.
Sometimes for light relief, I would go and stand out in the rain.

Her face didn't change when the hospital rang
to say he'd died. I remember them carrying him
downstairs on a stretcher. *Bye Grandad* I said.
He didn't answer. Perhaps he was back on the Somme.

Default

I can spread myself on the pavement, inflate like a cushion
>should any of them fall from a great height.

I will go without electricity if it means they can probe sockets
>safely with tiny outstretched fingers.

I can live without scissors, blunt every sharp instrument
>in case they take them, point upwards and run...

I will swim like a sea otter, float on my back, cradle them
>on my belly to keep them warm and dry;

dig a tunnel beneath that big tree, hole up with supplies
>until it's spring or after Brexit is done and Covid is gone –

I can do that.

I can put an ear to ice, listen for cracks and groans,
>bent double against katabatic winds,

become a bridge across sastrugi, sense a calving berg
>or ravenous bear by sniffing the air,

make fire with a glare if need be – cook hoosh
>from hardtack and pemmican,

kill a seal with my teeth, suck up blubber and blood,
>watch for danger with every frost-bitten step,

become magnetised with a sense of direction,
>find the way when all ways are north...

I can do that. It's easy.

Piano

Harriet's piano is still in the house where I used to live;
it's been there nine years longer than me now.
I bet he's never watered it or rubbed its wonderful wood
with beeswax, or paid a tuner to test its cold keys.
I bet he's never pulled out the tapestry-covered stool,
lifted its lid to check if the sheet music is still asleep
or even sat on it once.

I bet he won't remember if you lift the lid you can unfold
two brass candle holders from the days before electricity.
He won't know Dad used to sit there on Bank Holidays
bashing out tunes by ear, à la Les Dawson – glass of stout
placed precariously on the overpolished top, his butcher's hands
thumping up and down, he somehow managed
to hit more right notes than wrong.

Of course, you can have it back when you want he said,
having won another of those little victories.
Easier said than done, moving a piano across the country.
I dreamt the other day it descended from the sky
into my kitchen and I left it there by the island,
in case Dad wanted to come back, play to me in lockdown –
Memories are made of this or *I remember you;*
when he would wink at Mum and even throw in a yodel.

Overlap

this strangest week
we have all shifted up the family tree,
balancing on our branches, unsure of our footholds.
As if all the days on the calendar had been torn up,
thrown in the air today as we all change places –
move to the front of the bus as Dad used to say.

Now we are soaked in medical vocabulary
we don't like the sound of: *haemorrhage, ventilator,
infection.* Such grown-up words and I feel as far away
as the sun. No longer just a parent, I take the place of
she who fed chickens from her gathered-up apron,
arms wobbling just as mine do now.

I walk in the post-equinox sun; it's weak but bright.
I stop, sit on a bench like a cat in a sun-puddle.
From across the road a man calls over
  You've got the right spot there – take those last rays.
At my feet, a falling conker splits open like our baby girl,
red and shiny, coiled tight from the pickling of the womb,
squinting in suspicion and awe as her turn comes around.
Lifting my face to the sun, I will hold her today.

Eggs

She had a way with words, did Harriet. *Will you have it now,*
or when you get it? would muddle my young brain.
Let's get a wash; you never know who's coming
left me permanently expecting important visitors.
She smelled of mothballs, cooking and liquorice allsorts;
she let me walk the dog, feed chickens a mix of bran mashed
with hot tea leaves (*It makes the best eggs* she said),
and would warn with a look when he was in a bad mood.

Then we would retreat to the cold back room to set free
the Laughing Policeman on the gramophone. I would watch
the soft flesh of her arms move as she blew bubbles,
collected eggs, scrubbed the butcher's dirty laundry.
This month I am the age she was when she died.
The thud and thump of my two-ball against the wall
shifts in and out of focus, seems barely a blink away,
Eeneymeanymackaracka, rare-rye dominacka.

She sits like a brood hen on her wooden stool by the boiler,
watches me run between Chinese lanterns and lily of the valley,
on alert in case I venture too close to his prize-winning dahlias
or the strawberries that he counts before he goes to work.
It's mine now, that stool. I sit on it,
watch my granddaughter run wild in the garden.

Before the fall

Bathroom as hot as a sauna,
clean clothes finally found, bath run.
I tested the temperature as for my babies.
Later, she called for help getting out –
but with her voice as weak
                     as a pipit's
and my hearing half-disappeared, I didn't
hear her straight away. Just a minute or two,
but when I went in her tiny frame
                     was perched on the bath edge,
exhausted by the effort of trying to become vertical
with knees that wouldn't bend.
So I lifted her,
lifted my towel-wrapped mother,
arms around my shoulders,
shaking with pain no longer hidden.
Oh   she said *this is awful. Don't get this old, lovie.*
No, don't.

On not being a twin

I thought she might die that day in A&E where we all
converged, waited with her, held a hand.
Grey hair wild *like Einstein* she said, not realising
it was her when I showed her a picture later.
She lay so small, her face bruised from where
she had hit the sideboard on the way down.

A geriatric epidural brought blissful numbness
while they sorted out what was broken. Ninety-one,
and to say she'd the memory of a goldfish would be
a kindness, but as she looked around the tiny cubicle
it was enough to know we were there.

A doctor came in, asked *What's your name?*
She gave her maiden name from so long ago.
Do we have a queen or a king? She mustered
a disdainful look and said *The Queen* as if he was stupid.
Then, pointing to one of her identical twin sons
standing stiff with anxiety at the foot of the bed,
he said *And what's this gentleman's name?*
A momentary panic, in case she mixed them up.
They're my lovely boys she said.

Cocktails

choosing from the extensive menu
I'll have a dementia daiquiri
says the monster that sits on high
invisible straw pushed through her skull
sipping when it suits from this unholy cocktail
    a bit today
        a bit tomorrow

until finally   in the slush at the bottom   waiting to be sucked up
is the best bit   the thickest tastiest part
the part that knows who we are
where all the love that she has left is
it's a race   to keep that part as long as possible
until all that's left is the empty container   where she used to be
    and he shouts   *Get me another*
moves on

I must remind myself that this is a good thing

I haven't touched my son's son
              for twenty weeks, almost half his little life.
I've seen his face via photo, phone and Zoom,
seen his sister checking his temperature as he sits, stoic;
heard her say   *No Nonna, you mustn't touch.*
I've missed his squeaks as he tried to raise himself onto all fours,
his first tiny teethbuds showing themselves.
I cannot squeeze his little puck of a body
or hear that laugh that children are born with.

We have never been alone together
but I've seen at a distance his first copy clap,
his mastery of the royal wave, his marvellous Tintin quiff.
I must remind myself that this is a good thing,
more than many will ever have now.
But I ache for him to hold out his arms, to know the smell of me.
I want to not be that silver-haired person
who waves and smiles from a computer.
I try to imagine seeing my grandmothers just on a screen.
I can't.

A grandmother in isolation

I try to be upbeat when speaking to them
but I can't get rid of the feeling that this is karma –
personal and collective, perhaps punishment
for Bad Things I Must Have Done.
Everything has fallen off the edge of a cliff
and it's not even been six weeks. I wander about aimlessly.
The little train has stopped its hourly rhythm,
and there are no planes going down to Luton.

They FaceTimed me with the children
from the garden this morning.
I wasn't dressed, had no idea what time it was.
It was almost a shock to see them.
I have an actual pain in my heart.
Ava said   *Nonna, I really want to go to a cafe with you
and have cake.* I could hardly speak.

A government food parcel arrived today, which made me cry.
I cry a lot – at the Dad's Army theme tune or when I can't
open the childproof bottle of cough syrup
while wondering if this is *a* cough or *the* cough.
I feel made of paper some days, as if I might blow away.
Thank god Mum died. I could get it any day and die, alone,
without ever seeing or holding them again.
Perhaps I should prepare, scribble down a will,
but am not sure how.

I watch Aggie tell us *How to deep clean your house*
so I'm wiping handles and light switches every day
and there's no one here but me. I light a fire,
sit in the dark (to be authentic) and listen to *Wolf Hall* –
when you could leave home in the morning
and your whole family could be dead by teatime.
Thankfully we're not quite there yet. I cry, again.

Looking out of the window, nothing moves.
I wish the robin would come back and peer in at me.
He doesn't. I lean my forehead on the glass.

Red

There's a red kite
    whose patch encompasses my house.

I watch him most days, sweeping in slow circles,
    letting updrafts do the work for him,
        using his forked tail to steer the skies.

On the first day of lockdown,
    as I drew back the curtains to let the grey in,
        he was the first moving thing I saw.

So surprisingly low I could almost count splayed feathers
    on wingtips, eye on predatory eye as – just for a second –
        he seemed to peer into the bedroom.

I think we're quite close now;
    at least more than nodding acquaintances.

When it snowed I considered wearing red,
    curling up in the front garden
        to be as small as I felt.

He might think me carrion – perhaps swoop upon me,
    take me to his eyrie.
        His little ones could be surrogate for mine.

He could bring me small mammals I would learn to eat raw,
    my mouth and their little beaks
        red with the effort.

I could teach his nestlings songs from *Moana*, number rhymes,
    how to play Jacks with leftover vertebrae, then at sunset
        we'd screech their names to a bleeding sky
            and I would tell them how the world used
            to be.

Press me in peat

                let me sink into mud like those warrior women,
gold torc, rope noose or woven thong around my neck.
Let layers form above me, a shelter from wildfires
or melting glaciers. I could be discovered by peat cutters
or archaeologists who would investigate the calcium content
of my bones, examine food remnants in my stomach
then exclaim about my appalling diet.
They could posit theories on the arrangement of my limbs,
my bent little finger or the unhealed fracture in my foot,
never knowing it was from running up dark stairs
to a seedy Chinese restaurant in a Dublin back street
when we weren't getting on.

So, no burning or throwing of ashes into the wind.
Scatter bog myrtle and ivy flowers on me,
lay my phone nearby; a flask of tea, some Kit Kats,
and photos of you all.
Press me in peat.
Let my fingerprints remain intact and my skin turn to leather.
Let them wonder if I was sacrificed at Solstice
to stop global warming when all science has failed,
the bees are gone and the drugs don't work,
or if I just lay down, face to the sky,
on a bed of sphagnum moss because, like now,
I just couldn't bear it any more.

ACKNOWLEDGEMENTS

Thanks to all poets and friends who have got me this far.

A version of 'Before the fall' was placed second in Dementia UK's annual poetry competition in 2021.

ABOUT THE POET

Valerie Bence finished her doctorate in her mid-fifties and completed a Poetry MA at MMU in 2017. She was shortlisted for the Poetry School/Nine Arches Press Primers 4 in 2018, the Fish Poetry prize in 2019, and longlisted for the Ginkgo Prize in 2019. Her first collection, *Falling in love with a dead man*, was published by Cinnamon Press in 2019. She is a mum and nonna and lives and works in Buckinghamshire.

ABOUT THE EMMA PRESS

The Emma Press is an independent publishing house based in the Jewellery Quarter, Birmingham, UK. It was founded in 2012 by Emma Dai'an Wright, and specialises in poetry, short fiction and children's books.

In 2020 The Emma Press received funding from Arts Council England's Elevate programme, developed to enhance the diversity of the arts and cultural sector by strengthening the resilience of diverse-led organisations.

Website: theemmapress.com
Facebook, Twitter and Instagram: @TheEmmaPress